Using
MAPS

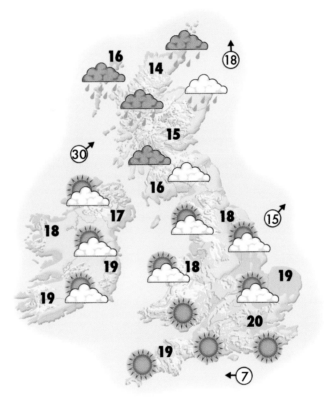

Jack and Meg Gillett

WAYLAND

First published in 2008 by Wayland

Copyright © Wayland 2008

Wayland
338 Euston Road
London NW1 3BH

Wayland Australia
Hachette Children's Books
Level 17/207 Kent Street
Sydney, NSW 2000

Managing Editor: Rasha Elsaeed
Editor: Katie Dicker
Picture researcher: Shelley Noronha
Designer: Alix Wood; Illustrator: Catherine Ward
Author dedication: 'For Beech House School'

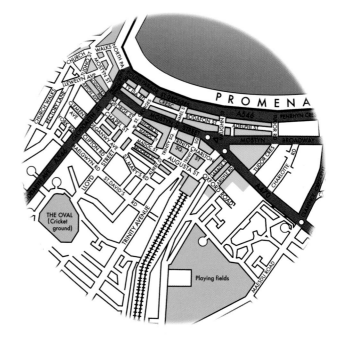

Picture Credits
Front cover, top left: Jack & Meg Gillett. Page 5; Page 11, Figure B; Page 18, bottom; Page 21: Reproduced by permission of Ordnance Survey on behalf of HMSO. © Crown copyright 2008. All rights reserved. Ordnance Survey Licence number 100047991. Page 7, Figure B: GMPTE. Page 8: Skyscan. Page 10, middle left/right, bottom left; Page 11, top right; Page 18, top right; Page 19, top/middle right; Page 20, Figure A; Page 23, middle left, top/middle right: Jack & Meg Gillett. Page 15: © Crown Copyright and/or database rights. Reproduced by permission of the Controller of Her Majesty's Stationery Office and the UK Hydrographic Office (www.ukho.gov.uk). Page 29: Adrian Warren/www.lastrefuge.co.uk.

Note to parents and teachers: Every effort has been made by the publishers to ensure that websites referred to in the book are suitable for children. However, because of the nature of the Internet, it is impossible to guarantee that the contents of these sites will not be altered. We strongly advise that Internet access is supervised by a responsible adult.

British Library Cataloguing in Publication Data
Gillett, Jack
  Using maps. – (Maps and mapping skills)
  1. Map reading – Juvenile literature 2. Cartography –
  Juvenile literature
  I. Title II. Gillett, Meg
  912'.014

ISBN 978 0 7502 5231 7

Printed in China

Wayland is a division of Hachette Children's Books, an Hachette Livre UK Company www.hachettelivre.co.uk

Contents

Maps at work

Maps aren't just for geography students. They're a great help to anyone who enjoys outdoor activities. Maps are essential to many industries, too. Lorry drivers, for example, use maps to find their way around road **networks** to deliver their goods.

Hi-tech mapping

A **Global Positioning System** (G.P.S.) is a hi-tech form of mapping that people often use to find their way around (Figure A). Unfortunately, G.P.S. isn't always reliable so it's still important to be able to read a traditional map.

Maps for building

People in the construction (building) industry use maps and plans in many stages of their work. Figure B shows some important examples.

▲ A G.P.S. receiver monitors signals from satellites orbiting the Earth to pinpoint its exact location. G.P.S. is often used in vehicles to plan routes.

B

1. Surveyors choose a suitable site to build on, and map it in great detail.

2. Architects draw plans of the new buildings to go on the site.

3. Builders use plans to construct the walls of the buildings, and then tile their roofs.

4. Engineers lay pipes and cables. These are drawn on site maps so they can be located for repair work later on.

Do it yourself

1 Figure C shows a map of Launceston, a small town in Cornwall. It also shows four numbered sites that could be used to build a new housing estate. Use this map to answer the five questions in the table below – write 'Yes' or 'No' in each blank space on your own copy of the table.

2 a Which of the sites is the most suitable to build on (has the most 'yes' answers)?

b Look at the map again, to see if you can find an even better site for the estate. If you can, give its six-figure grid reference **location** and suggest reasons why it is such a good site.

	Site 1	Site 2	Site 3	Site 4
Away from a main road, so little noise and pollution?				
Away from a river, so safe from flooding?				
Close to a road, so has easy access by car?				
On flat land, so easy to build on?				
Within 0.5 km of a school, so not far for children to walk?				
Total number of 'Yes' answers				

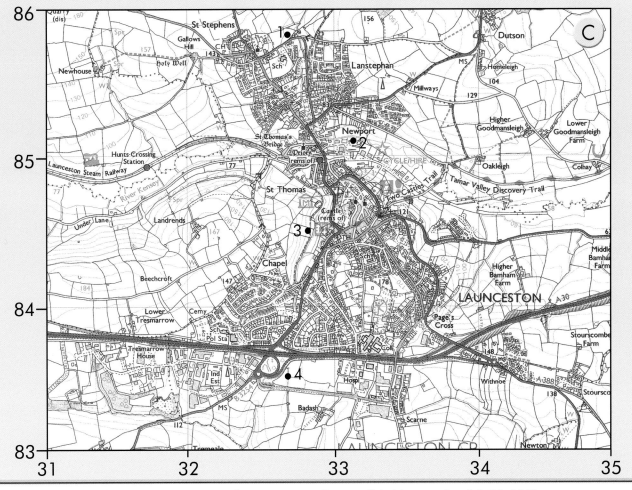

▲ An Ordnance Survey map of Launceston, Cornwall (with a scale of 1:25,000).

Topological maps

Topographical maps provide a wide range of information about the physical and human features of an area. But there are other maps, called **topological maps**, which just show links between places. One of the best examples is the map of the London Underground system.

Topological maps show networks – the patterns made by places and the transport links between them (Figure B). Topological maps look different to 'ordinary' maps. For this reason, people often think they're diagrams, not real maps at all!

Accurate distances and directions aren't important on topological maps, which is why their **routes** can be drawn as straight lines. Passengers on Manchester's Metrolink network, for example, don't need to know how far apart the stations are – just when and where to get on and off the trams (Figure C).

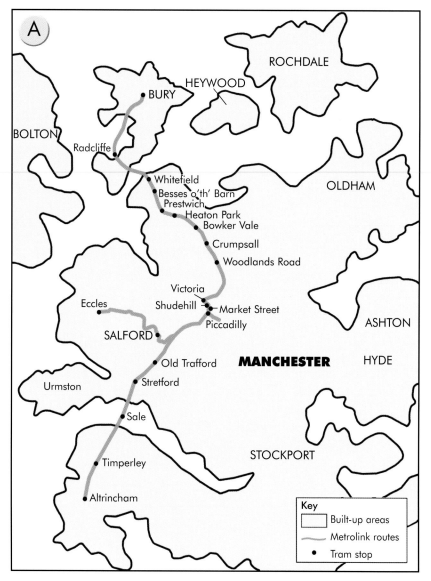

▲ A topographical map of Greater Manchester and its Metrolink network. The map shows the extent of this urban area.

Do it yourself

1 Mrs Williams lives exactly 3 minutes walk from Radcliffe Metrolink station. She works in the city centre, only 2 minutes walk from Market Street station. She starts work at 8:30 am, but likes to get there by 8:20 am. Using the tram timetable below, what is the latest time she can leave home to be sure of getting into work by 8:20 am?

2 Mrs Williams needs to be home this evening by 4 pm, to attend an event at her son's school. Assuming the return tram journey takes exactly the same time, when should she leave work to be sure of getting home on time?

3 Draw your own route from home to school as a topological map. It will have a single, straight line, with your friends' houses and any other places you pass drawn (and labelled) at equally-spaced distances.

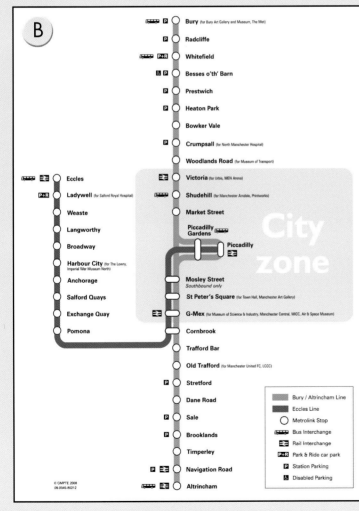

B

Bury (for Bury Art Gallery and Museum, The Met)
Radcliffe
Whitefield
Besses o'th' Barn
Prestwich
Heaton Park
Bowker Vale
Crumpsall (for North Manchester Hospital)
Woodlands Road (for Museum of Transport)
Victoria (for Urbis, MEN Arena)
Shudehill (for Manchester Arndale, Printworks)
Market Street
Piccadilly Gardens
Piccadilly
Mosley Street *Southbound only*
St Peter's Square (for Town Hall, Manchester Art Gallery)
G-Mex (for Museum of Science & Industry, Manchester Central, MICC, Air & Space Museum)
Cornbrook
Trafford Bar
Old Trafford (for Manchester United FC, LCCC)
Stretford
Dane Road
Sale
Brooklands
Timperley
Navigation Road
Altrincham

Eccles
Ladywell (for Salford Royal Hospital)
Weaste
Langworthy
Broadway
Harbour City (for The Lowry, Imperial War Museum North)
Anchorage
Salford Quays
Exchange Quay
Pomona

City zone

© GMPTE 2008
08-0045-80212

Legend:
Bury / Altrincham Line
Eccles Line
○ Metrolink Stop
Bus Interchange
Rail Interchange
P+R Park & Ride car park
P Station Parking
Disabled Parking

▲ A topological map of Manchester's Metrolink network.

C METROLINK

First train to Manchester Piccadilly leaves from:-	At:-
Bury	06.00
Radcliffe	06.02
Whitefield	06.05
Besses o'th' Barn	06.06
Prestwich	06.08
Heaton Park	06.10
Bowker Vale	06.12
Crumpsall	06.14
Woodlands Road	06.16
Victoria Station	06.22
Shudehill	06.24
Market Street	06.25
Piccadilly	06.30

Then every 12 minutes until 07.15
Then every 6 minutes

▲ A weekday timetable of Manchester's Metrolink network between Bury and Piccadilly stations.

National Parks

National Parks are special places. Government laws protect their beautiful **landscapes** for everyone to enjoy. These laws prevent the building of large housing developments or factories that could pollute the natural **environment**.

Britain's National Parks

Figure A shows the locations of Britain's National Parks. Each park is different because of its own, unique scenery. Britain's largest park is the Cairngorms (below), in the mountains of northern Scotland; the smallest, the Norfolk Broads, is ten times smaller and is on some of the lowest, flattest land in Britain.

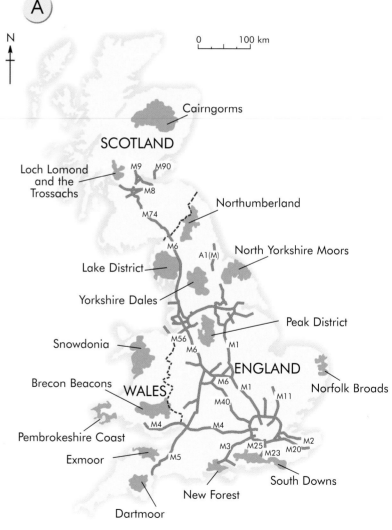

▲ A view of Cairngorms National Park in Scotland – Britain's largest National Park.

▲ A map of Britain's National Parks and motorways.

Do it yourself

1 Use Figure A to complete a copy of this table:

Country	Number of National Parks in each country
England	
Scotland	
Wales	
Total number of National Parks in Britain	

2 According to Figures A, B and C, which of these statements about Britain's National Parks are true:

a Most of them are in upland areas.
b Most of them are in sparsely-populated areas.

c Over half of them are on the coast.
d The Peak District is the only park to have cities to its west, south and east.

3 Use these three websites to discover the ways in which the Lake District and the Norfolk Broads National Parks are:

a similar to each other.

b different from each other.

http://www.countryside.gov.uk/LAR/Landscape/DL/national_parks/index.asp
www.fatbadgers.co.uk/Britain/natparks.htm
www.nationalparks.gov.uk

B

Key
- Over 200 metres
- Under 200 metres

North West Highlands
Grampian Mountains
Southern Uplands
Cumbrian Mountains
Pennines
North Yorks Moors
Yorkshire Wolds
Snowdonia
The Cotswolds
The Chilterns
Exmoor
North Downs
South Downs
Bodmin Moor
Dartmoor

0   100 km

▲ A map showing the height of the land in Britain.

C

Key
- Over 150 people per square km
- 10-150 people per square km
- Under 10 people per square km
- Capital cities
- Other major cities

SCOTLAND
Scottish Highlands
Glasgow
Edinburgh
Newcastle-Upon-Tyne
Lake District
Pennines
Leeds
Manchester
Liverpool
Sheffield
Cambrian Mts
Nottingham
Birmingham
ENGLAND
WALES
Cardiff
London
Bristol
Southampton

0   100 km

▲ A population density map of Britain.

How to follow a route

Many people explore the British countryside by following a national network of walks or pathways. Others prefer to follow routes recommended by clubs or organisations. Route guides often assume that walkers can follow routes easily. Try out the following activities to test your own skills!

1 Follow these route instructions using the O.S. map on page 11, which shows a part of the North Yorkshire coast:

   a Start at the Visitor Centre in Ravenscar (979 017).

▲ Ravenscar Visitor Centre.

   b Go south-east along Station Road for about 100 m, then turn north-north-east and walk along a part of the Long Distance Walk (Trail) called the Cleveland Way for 300 m. This takes you to the cliff edge, where you turn east-south-east.

◀ One of the signposts along the Cleveland Way.

   c Follow the Cleveland Way, in a generally south-east direction, along the cliff top, for about 2.5 km.

▲ Part of the Cleveland Way near to Common Cliff. The building is an old coastguard lookout post.

   d Turn off the Cleveland Way at War Dike Gate, then walk in a south-west direction for 150 m.

   e Turn south-south-east, then walk down War Dike Lane for 400 m. This brings you to the start of the footpath leading to Meeting House Farm.

2 Write a similar set of instructions for walkers who want to get back to the Visitor Centre, but using a different route which takes them past the following places: the ford across a stream (Figure A); Meeting House Farm; the western edge of Sandybed Wood; Grange Farm; Bell Hill Farm; Danesdale; Bent Rigg Lane; Church Road Farm.

◀ This ford is 0.2 km north-east of Meeting House Farm.

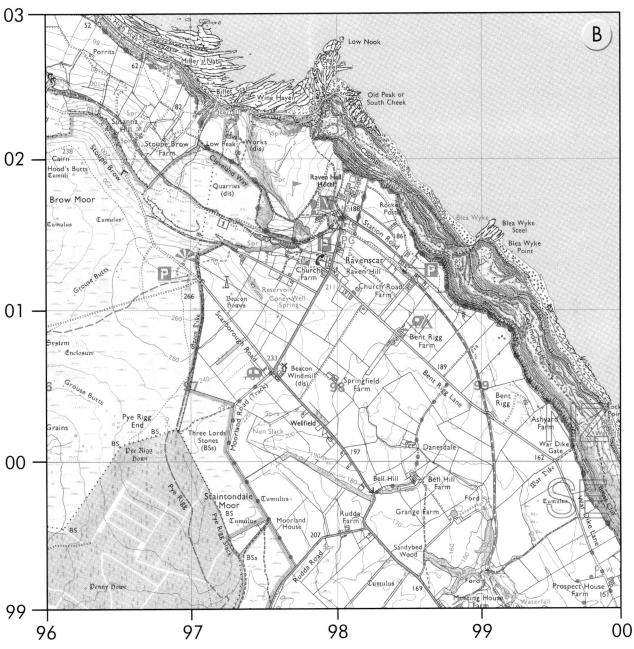

▲ An O.S. map of the Ravenscar area (with a scale of 1:25,000).

Weather maps

The weather in the British Isles can change from day to day. Forecasting (predicting) future weather has never been easy, but satellites help **weather forecasters** to do this more accurately. They use satellites to 'see' the movement of weather patterns nearby.

The British Isles lie between the Atlantic Ocean (which creates damp air) and Europe (which can be very hot in summer, but very cold in winter). Satellites track weather systems, but weather forecasters also use instruments to monitor changes in temperature, wind direction, wind speed and air pressure. They use this information to draw **synoptic charts** (Figure A).

Synoptic charts show a lot of detailed information, so the **Meteorological Office** produces a simpler version for people to see at a glance what the weather will be like (Figure B). Written forecasts can also be viewed online (on the BBC website for example). Spoken versions of the weather forecast are also broadcast in regular television and radio news bulletins.

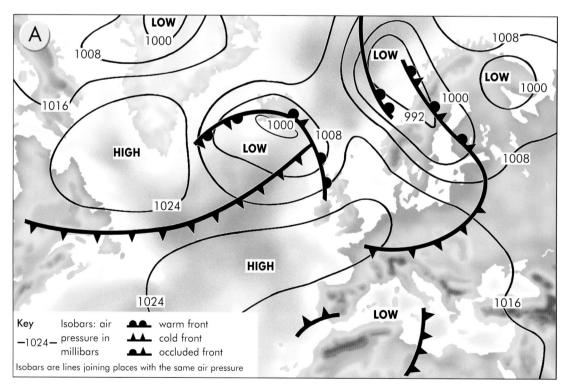

▲ The synoptic chart showing air pressure and weather fronts.

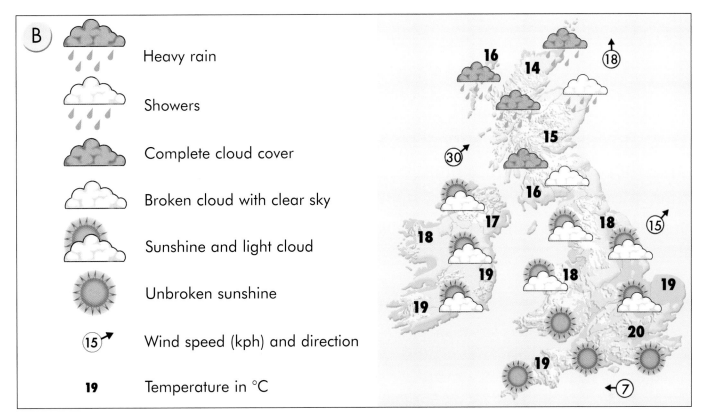

B

Symbol	Meaning
Heavy rain
Showers
Complete cloud cover
Broken cloud with clear sky
Sunshine and light cloud
Unbroken sunshine
⑮ ↗	Wind speed (kph) and direction
19	Temperature in °C

▲ A weather forecast map interpreting the synoptic chart in Figure A.

Do it yourself

1 Look at today's weather conditions on **www.bbc.co.uk/weather/ukweather** (Click on 'visible satellite'). What's the weather like? Clear skies on the satellite image may indicate a sunny day, but lots of cloud probably means lots of rain!

2 a Use the BBC weather site (or a similar website) to find the daily weather forecast. Do this every day for a week and display the information you get in a copy of the table below. Look at the examples of the kinds of entries you might add to each cell.

b Record the accuracy of each day's forecast by shading the cells green for 'accurate' and red for 'wrong'.

c Were these forecasts accurate enough to be considered 'reliable'?

	Temperature	Cloud cover	Rainfall	Wind strength	Wind direction
Monday					
Tuesday					
Wednesday					
Thursday					
Friday					
Saturday					
Sunday					

Examples: Very warm, Really cold, Clear skies, Very cloudy, Light showers, Heavy rain, Calm, Windy, From the south-west

Navigation charts

Maps of seas and harbours are called navigation charts. They are created when **survey** ships plot the depth of the seabed (Figure A). Submarine (underwater) contours then show this information in metres. Navigation charts are invaluable to sailors in unfamiliar waters.

Shallow depths

Dangerous coastal waters less than 20 metres deep also have 'spot depths', given to the nearest tenth of a metre. For example, 7_4 stands for 7.4 m. Shallow water is especially dangerous to ships, so it is coloured to make it stand out. These areas often have shipwrecks which are marked on charts by the letters Wk.

Figure B is part of a British Admiralty navigation chart. You can see sandbanks and deep and shallow water. It also shows part of the large compass rose used by sailors. It is divided into 360 degrees – a more accurate way of steering ships than using compass directions such as north-west. Degrees are also used to plot the **bearings** of a ship's position on a chart.

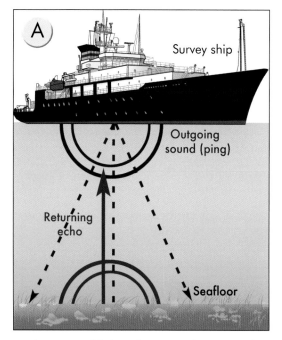

▲ A survey ship's echo-sounder at work. The depth of the water is worked out by calculating how long it takes the signal to return to the ship.

Do it yourself

Use the map in Figure B to answer the following questions:

1. a How high is the highest point on Puffin Island?
    b What is the greatest depth of water in the Pool, in the centre of the chart?

2. What colour shadings on British Admiralty charts are used to show:
    a deep water (over 5 m deep)?
    b land which is always above sea level?
    c sandbanks and beaches which are covered at high tide?
    d shallow water (less than 5 m deep)?

3. Why is the safe shipping channel between Anglesey and Puffin Island not exactly half-way between them?

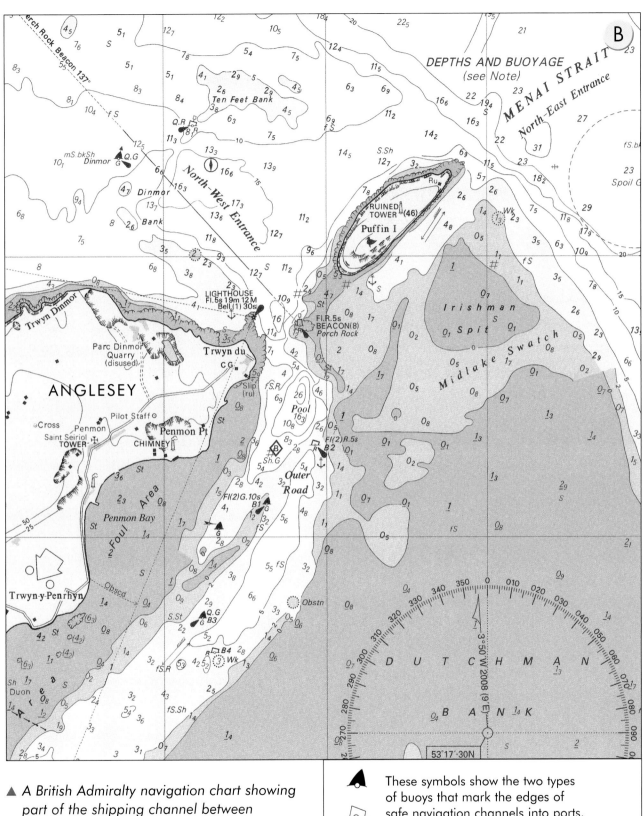

▲ A British Admiralty navigation chart showing part of the shipping channel between Anglesey and the Welsh mainland.

These symbols show the two types of buoys that mark the edges of safe navigation channels into ports.

Road atlases

Road atlases have maps showing different kinds of roads as well as the towns they link. Drivers use these atlases to find their way around. Information about journey times and speeds also helps drivers to decide which route to take.

A trip to Llandudno

A group of Year 5 and 6 pupils from Birmingham is going on a fieldwork trip to Llandudno. Some of these pupils use a road atlas to find out how to get there.

The distance chart in their atlas (Figure A) shows the distance in kilometres between major towns and cities. The chart shows that Birmingham and Llandudno are 221 km apart. However, it doesn't tell the pupils how long it takes to get there, or which way to go!

Their atlas map (Figure B) shows that there are many routes from Birmingham to Llandudno. Their teacher tells them to choose any four routes and search the Internet to find out more about them. Figure C shows what they discovered.

Aberdeen									
685	Birmingham								
850	175	Cardiff							
237	467	632	Glasgow						
573	159	234	352	Liverpool					
665	221	310	447	99	Llandudno				
867	191	245	646	342	383	London			
563	140	305	342	60	130	321	Manchester		
817	256	439	603	407	450	184	300	Norwich	
997	321	245	775	472	513	346	451	541	Plymouth

◀ A road atlas distance chart showing the distance (in km) between Birmingham and Llandudno.

Do it yourself

1 Use a road atlas to make your own distance chart like the one in Figure A. It must include the nearest town to where you live, but you can choose the other places. You could colour all the chart distances from your nearest town.

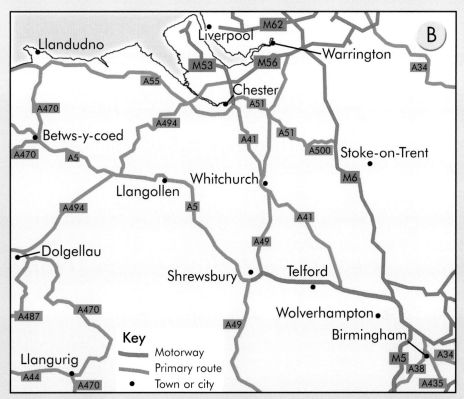

▲ *A road atlas map showing the routes between Birmingham and Llandudno.*

2 Use Figures B and C to decide which route in the table you would choose:

a to drive the shortest distance between Birmingham and Llandudno.

b to get to Llandudno as quickly as possible.

c to be able to stop at lots of motorway service stations.

3 Use the following website to produce a table like the one in Figure C for three different routes between your home town and another place you would like to visit.
http://theaa.com/travelwatch/inc/planner_places_redirect.jsp?unit=true

Route	Places visited between Birmingham and Llandudno	Distance (in km)	Time taken (in minutes)	Average speed (in km per hour)
A	Shrewsbury, Llangollen, Betws-y-Coed	210.3	177	71.3
B	Whitchurch, Chester	195.2	166	70.6
C	Stoke-on-Trent, Chester	208.7	177	72.8
D	Stoke-on-Trent, Warrington, Chester	230.3	159	86.9

▲ *Information about the routes between Birmingham and Llandudno.*

Llandudno's history

(A)

Llandudno is a **holiday resort** on the North Wales coast, only 5 km from the beautiful mountain landscapes of the Snowdonia National Park.
It is built on a low, flat coastal ridge (called a **tombolo**), between two **bays** and two **headlands**.

▲ *Miners' cottages on the steep slopes of the Great Orme.*

One of these limestone headlands, the Great Orme, was mined for copper by the Romans and the Vikings. The cottages up its steep side (Figure A) belonged to the copper miners. These clusters of cottages are the oldest buildings in Llandudno.

During the 1800s, people thought that sea bathing greatly improved their health. Places like Blackpool, Brighton and Llandudno grew rapidly to cater for the visiting bathers – especially after they were linked to the national railway network. Llandudno was planned as a **new town**, which is why most of its streets are straight or gently curving. Its seafront was lined with big hotels, and its new pier became a popular holiday attraction. Figure C shows that Llandudno's population was 30 times larger in 1901 than it was in 1801!

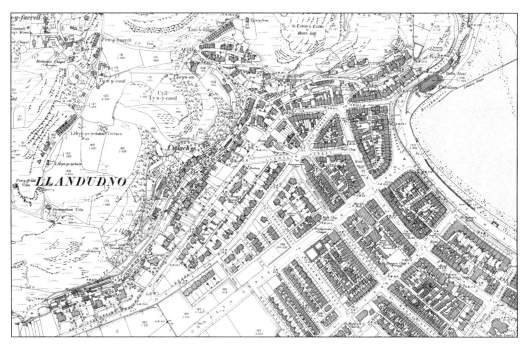

▲ *This historic map shows Llandudno in 1900. The miners' cottages were located at Tan-y-stage (top middle).*

Do it yourself

1 Use Figure C to discover the four years when Llandudno's population reached 5, 10, 15 and 20 thousand people.

2 Use this website to find the years when these events took place: **http://en.wikipedia.org/wiki/Llandudno**
  a pier built
  b railway station opened
  c Artificial Ski Slope and Toboggan Run opened
  d Great Orme Cabin Lift built
  e Happy Valley Park given to the town by Lord Mostyn to commemorate Queen Victoria's Golden Jubilee
  f Professor Codman's first Punch and Judy show.

▲ *St. George's Hotel – Llandudno's first big hotel.*

3 Use your answers to Activities 1 and 2 to complete an enlarged copy of the timeline below. Do this by adding the three missing lines and the ten missing years.

▲ *Llandudno Promenade and Pier.*

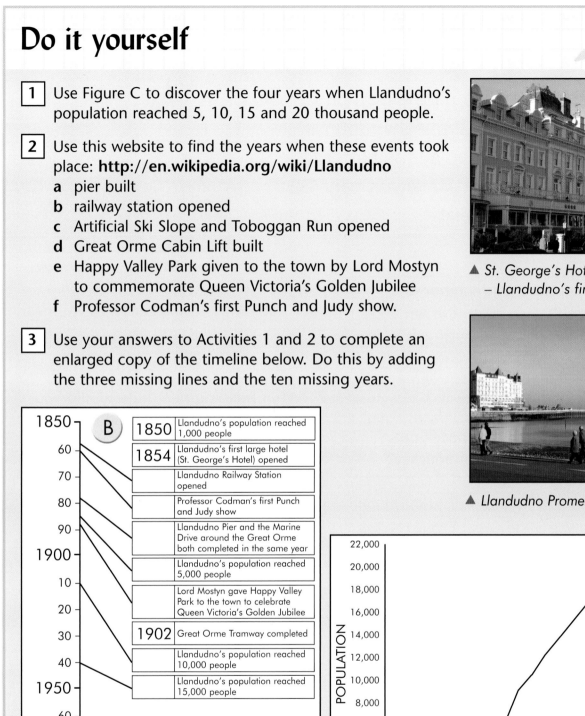

	B	
1850	1850	Llandudno's population reached 1,000 people
60	1854	Llandudno's first large hotel (St. George's Hotel) opened
70		Llandudno Railway Station opened
80		Professor Codman's first Punch and Judy show
90		Llandudno Pier and the Marine Drive around the Great Orme both completed in the same year
1900		Llandudno's population reached 5,000 people
10		
20		Lord Mostyn gave Happy Valley Park to the town to celebrate Queen Victoria's Golden Jubilee
30	1902	Great Orme Tramway completed
40		Llandudno's population reached 10,000 people
1950		Llandudno's population reached 15,000 people
60		
70		Great Orme Cabin Lift opened
80		Artificial Ski Slope and Toboggan Run both opened in the same year
90		
2000		Llandudno's population reached 20,000 people

▲ *A timeline showing key events in Llandudno's history.*

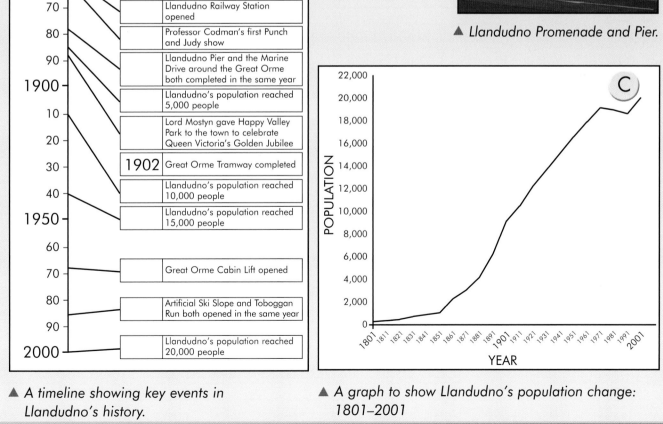

▲ *A graph to show Llandudno's population change: 1801–2001*

Use your skills: Exploring Llandudno

This 'quiz tour' is based on the map on page 21. It helped the Birmingham pupils to get to know Llandudno a little better (see pages 16-17). Use the key on page 32 to help you to do the quiz!

▲ Llandudno's tramway terminus.

You're in the **traffic** that's entering the map area from the south, on the A470 main road. You then travel north-east along the B5115 secondary road, and turn off it onto the road which takes you past the Bus and Coach Station.

1   How many roundabouts have you passed on this part of your journey?

You get off the coach and walk along the same road towards the Great Orme.

2   What kind of 'place of worship' do you walk past on the right side of this road?

3   Why does this long road curve gently, instead of being dead-straight?

You walk to the end of the pier.

4   What direction are you walking in on your way back?

You then go the short distance to the Cable Car Station.

5   What four-figure grid square are you now in?

Your ride on the cable car takes you near to the highest place on the Great Orme.

6   What is the '**spot height**' of this place?

7   What building near here would you go to get information about the Great Orme?

You return to Llandudno, but on the tramway this time.

8   What is the six-figure grid reference of the last tramway station which you come to? (see Figure A).

You come to the main road that links Llandudno's two bays.

9   How long would it take you to walk the distance between its two sharp bends if your speed was 4 km per hour?

Finally, you walk around the streets in grid square 7781.

10 How would the buildings you see be different from those in square 7882?

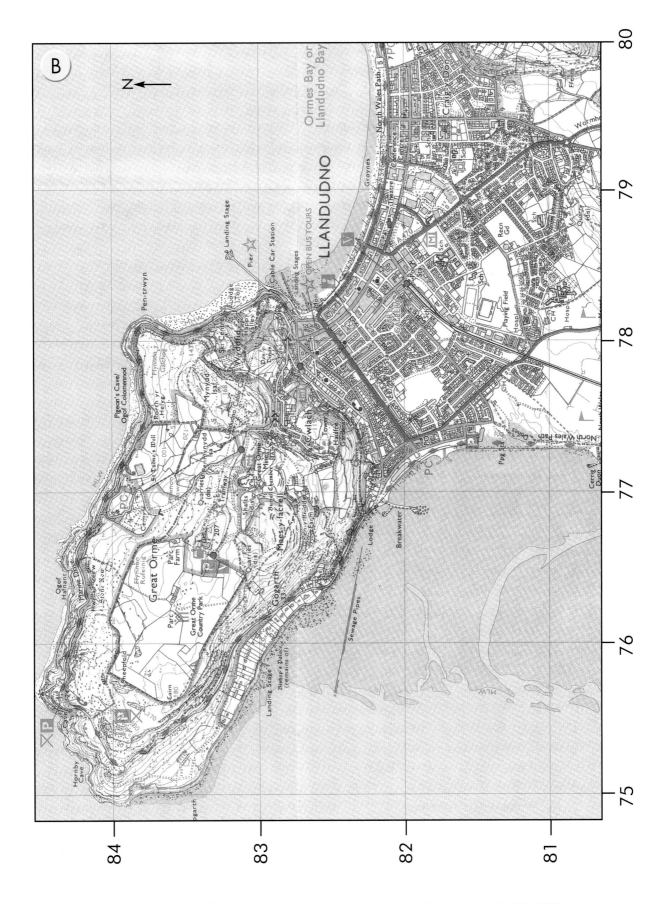

▲ *An O.S. map of modern Llandudno and the Great Orme (with a scale of 1:25,000).*

Land use in Llandudno

The Birmingham pupils also investigated land use in Llandudno. They wanted to find out how the town's buildings and open spaces are used. They looked at the heart of the town – in particular its **Central Business District** (C.B.D.).

The research for this survey was carried out by recording the ground floor land use of every building shown in the **street plan** in Figure A. The land use codes used for buildings, and open spaces such as car parks, are listed in Figure B. This shows that shops are the most important type of land use in the survey area. It also shows which land uses can be described as services.

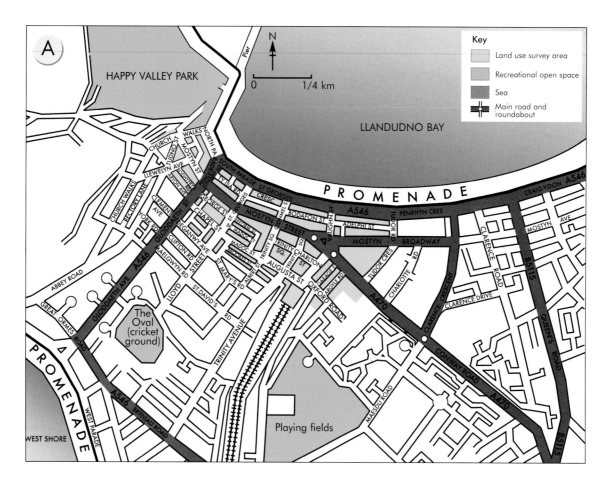

▲ *The area of Llandudno investigated by the Birmingham pupils (shaded in yellow).*

Do it yourself

B	% of properties with this land use	'Service' land use?	Examples of this type of land use
Shops	47	Yes	Newsagents, shoe shops
Offices	14	Yes	Accountants, solicitors
Residential	11	No	Flats, houses
Catering	10	Yes	Cafés, take-aways
Vacant properties	6	No	Empty shops, properties being rebuilt
Hotels	3	Yes	Guest houses, hotels
Industry	3	No	Car repair garages, printers
Public buildings	2	Yes	Museums, the Town Hall
Entertainment	2	Yes	Amusement arcades, cinemas
Car parks	2	Yes	Car parks

▲ Mostyn Broadway – Llandudno's longest and busiest shopping street.

▲ The Town Hall – one of Llandudno's largest 'public buildings'.

◄ A modern shopping centre at the southeastern end of Mostyn Broadway.

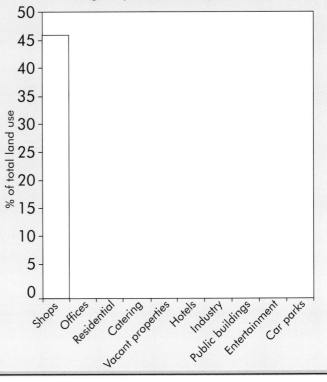

1 Suggest reasons why the three words of the term 'Central Business District' are so suitable for the part of the town they describe.

2 Use the information in Figure B to complete your own copy of this bar graph. Shade all the bars for the 'service' land uses one colour, but use a different colour for all the other uses. Complete the key to show the meanings of the two colours you have used to shade the bars.

3 Describe the main findings of the land use survey that are shown by your completed graph.

Key | ☐ 'Service' land uses | ☐ 'Non-service' land uses

% of total land use

50
45
40
35
30
25
20
15
10
5
0

Shops Offices Residential Catering Vacant properties Hotels Industry Public buildings Entertainment Car parks

Land use maps

There was another reason why the Birmingham pupils surveyed Llandudno's central area: they wanted to draw a land use map of it. They hoped it would show them where the town's Central Business District finished. Their completed map is shown on page 25.

Their map shows some interesting patterns. As they had expected, most of the big stores like Marks and Spencer, Woolworths and W.H. Smith are located on the main shopping street, Mostyn Street (below). This street was named after the rich family who owned the land which the new town of Llandudno was built on over 100 years ago. The pupils also discovered that there is a modern indoor shopping centre – the Victoria Centre – on the same street.

One pattern that the pupils hadn't expected was that some kinds of business seem to 'cluster' together.

▲ Mostyn Street has some of Llandudno's largest shops.

Do it yourself

1 Carry out a similar land use survey of a small town in your local area.

2 Use the information you have collected to:
a discover if any kinds of business such as banks and estate agents cluster together.
b locate the boundary line of this town's Central Business District.

All Llandudno's banks are located very near to each other. Guess where? Yes, on Mostyn Street! Most of the offices used by the town's solicitors and accountants also cluster together in the same way – this time around Trinity Square.

Their completed map also helped to give the pupils the answer they wanted: it is possible to find out where the C.B.D. ends, because the land use there changes so clearly. Its boundary line is shown by the thick, black line in Figure A.

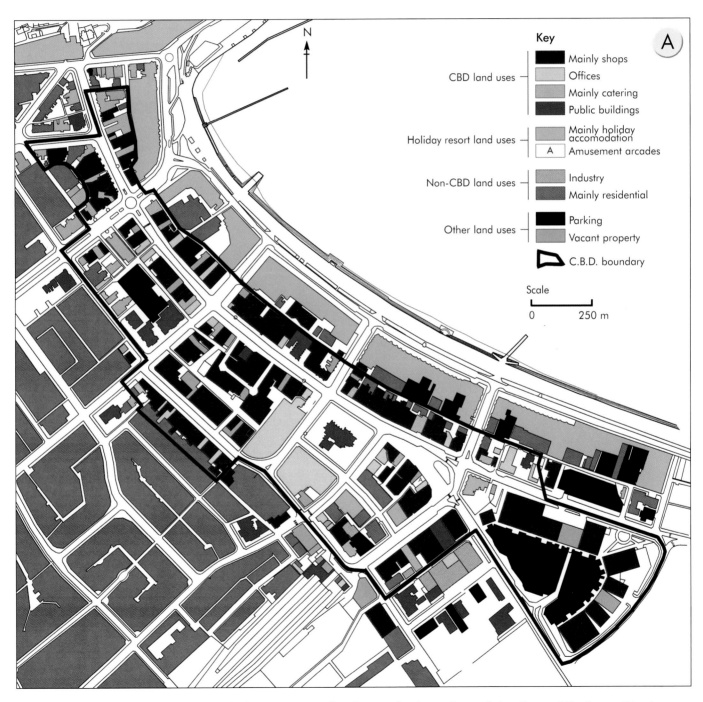

▲ A land use map of central Llandudno. You can clearly see the boundary of the Central Business District.

The Birmingham pupils designed a short
questionnaire (Figure A) for a survey of visitors to
Llandudno. Its last three questions were only put to
people who were **tourists** who lived in the British Isles
(but not to overseas visitors and local residents).

LLANDUDNO VISITOR SURVEY

Question 1
Do you live in or very near to
Llandudno, or are you a visitor to
the town?
- If the answer is 'I live in or very near
  to Llandudno', say: "Thank you, but
  my questionnaire is only for visitors.
  Good-bye!"
- If the answer is 'I am a visitor', say:
  "Thank you! Please could you
  answer the next three questions?"

Question 2
Are you in Llandudno:
- just for a one-day visit? or
- for an overnight stay?

Question 3
Did you get to Llandudno:
- by car? or
- by bus or coach? or
- by train?

Question 4
Which area on this map do you live in?

The answers to Questions 2 to 4 were
then added together. Their totals were
written in the tables shown in Figure B.

Do it yourself

1 Imagine that you are part of the group visiting Llandudno. Your task is to show the information in the tables opposite in a different way, by completing copies of the graphs and map in Figure B.

2 Write at least two useful facts about each completed graph and map you have drawn.

Type(s) of visit	Number of visitors
One-day	88
Overnight	12
Both types	100

▲ Information from survey question 2.

Type(s) of transport	Number of visitors
Car	75
Bus/coach	19
Train	6
All types	100

▲ Information from survey question 3.

Region in Britain	Number of visitors from the region
East Anglia	3
East Midlands	8
Northern England	10
Northern Ireland	3
North-West England	23
Republic of Ireland	5
Scotland	3
South-East England	13
South-West England	2
Wales	15
West Midlands	8
Yorkshire/Humberside	7
All regions	100

▲ Information from survey question 4.

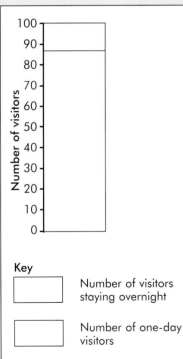

Key

☐ Number of visitors staying overnight

☐ Number of one-day visitors

Complete the graph by using two different colours to shade the two boxes in the key and the two parts of the bar.

Key

🚗 Car

☐ Bus/coach

☐ Train

Complete the graph by drawing a bus and train in the two blank boxes in the key, then using the same drawings (or part-drawings) in the two blank columns.

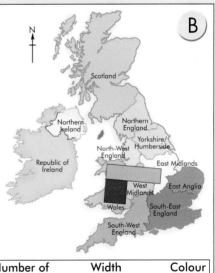

Number of visitors	Width of line	Colour of line
1-5	2 mm	Yellow
6-10	4 mm	Orange
11-15	6 mm	Red
over 15	8 mm	Purple

Complete the map by drawing a straight flow-line from Llandudno to the centre of each UK region shown in the table above. East Midlands and Wales have been completed for you!

Use your skills: Crossword

Make a photocopy of this page and use the clues to complete the crossword. Clue 6 across has been added to get you started! The numbers in brackets show how many letters are in each correct word (or words).

Clues for words across the crossword:

2   A city on the road between Birmingham and Llandudno. (7)

6   Any way of earning money. (8 + 8)

7   Vehicles moving on a road. (7)

8   A way of getting new information about a place. (6)

10 A line on a synoptic chart that links places having the same air pressure. (6)

12 Llandudno is built on one of these. (7)

13 Another word for a walking route. (5)

14 A type of map used by sailors and weather forecasters. (5)

16 Hard rock which the feature in the photograph is made of. (9)

17 Abbreviation for the company which produces 1:50,000 and 1:25,000 scale maps of the UK. (2)

19 Everything you can see around you! (9)

21 A type of rail transport used in Llandudno and Manchester. (4)

22 Llandudno's … was built in 1878. (4)

25 Second word in the name of the feature in the photograph. (4)

26 Llandudno is on the shore of the Irish … (3)

28 An area which has beautiful mountain landscapes and is only 5 km from Llandudno. (9)

31 The most common type of building in any town centre. (4)

32 Llandudno has two of these coastal features – one on each side. (7)

33 ……… to Llandudno became much better after the A55 main road along the North Wales coast was widened into a dual-carriageway. (6)

Clues for words down the crossword:

1   First word of the name of the feature shown in the photograph. (5)

2   Steep slopes all round the edge of the headland shown in the photograph. (6)

3   A line joining places on a journey. (5)

4   Where a place is. (8)

5   Map showing a town's main roads. (6 + 4)

8   First three letters of a word meaning 'under the sea'. (3)

9   A prediction of future weather. (8)

11 These all help to meet people's needs. (8)

15 A type of transport network that linked Llandudno to other places after 1846. (7)

18 Snowdonia and the Cairngorms are both this kind of park. (8)

20 A book of maps. (5)

23 Un-jumble the letters SAMRON to name these early visitors to North Wales! (6)

24 Llandudno was planned as an example of this type of town. (3)

26 1:25,000 is the ….. of the Ordnance Survey maps in this book. (5)

27 Metal ore mined by the Vikings. (6)

29 These are used to show sailors where the deepest, safest water is. (5)

30 Three-letter abbreviation for the heart of a town or city. (3)

Glossary

Bay A curved inlet of the sea.

Bearing A compass direction shown as a number of degrees clockwise from North.

Central Business District The centre of a town or city, where most of its shops and offices are sited. The words Central Business District are often shortened to C.B.D.

Distance chart A chart which shows distances between places on maps.

Environment Everything that is in a location – including all its air, land and water features.

Global Positioning System (G.P.S.) A high-tech system of mapping that uses satellites to pinpoint locations on Earth.

Headland Land which juts out into the sea.

Holiday resort A place that is very popular with holiday-makers and day-trippers.

Landscape What you can see around you.

Location The place where a feature is or where an activity takes place.

Meteorological Office The UK's national weather service (now called the Met Office).

National Park A beautiful area protected by laws to restrict building or industry.

Network A system of routes such as roads which link places together.

New town A modern town built to a carefully designed plan.

Questionnaire A series of questions asked as a way of collecting information for a survey.

Road atlas A book of maps showing different roads as well as the towns they link.

Route A journey line between two places.

Spot height The height of a place above sea level. Maps often show the spot heights of hilltops and places along roads.

Street plan A town map showing streets, street names and important buildings.

Survey The collection and recording of research information. Questionnaires can be used to interview people as part of a survey.

Synoptic chart A special map used by weather forecasters to show weather patterns.

Tombolo A long, narrow ridge of sand or shingle that joins an island to the mainland next to it.

Topological map A map that shows links between places, such as a map of railway routes and stations.

Tourist A person who spends holiday-time away from home.

Traffic The movement of bicycles and motor vehicles along a road.

Weather forecaster Someone who predicts what the weather will be like in the near future. A forecast might include air temperature, wind speed and any chance of rain, snow, sleet or hail falling.

Index and answers

Answers

p5 1) Site 1: Away from main road – yes. Away from a river – yes. Close to a road – yes. On flat land – yes. Within 0.5 km of a school – yes. Total number of yes answers – 5. Site 2: Away from main road – yes. Away from a river – no. Close to a road – yes. On flat land – yes. Within 0.5 km of a school – no. Total number of yes answers – 3. Site 3: Away from main road – yes. Away from a river – yes. Close to a road – no. On flat land – no. Within 0.5 km of a school – no. Total number of yes answers – 2. Site 4: Away from main road – no. Away from a river – yes. Close to a road – yes. On flat land – yes. Within 0.5 km of a school – no. Total number of yes answers – 3. **2a)** Site 1. **p7 1)** 07:47 (or 7:47 am). **2)** 15:25 (or 3:25 pm) – as the journey takes 28 minutes and she needs to allow up to 6 minutes in case she just misses a tram. **p9 1)** England: 10; Scotland: 2; Wales: 3; Total 15. **2)** All four are true. **p14 1a)** 46 m; **b)** 26 m **2a)** white **b)** yellow **c)** green **d)** blue. **3)** Because the deepest water is nearer to Anglesey than to Puffin Island. **p17 2a)** B **b)** D **c)** D. **p19 1)** 5,000 in approx 1885; 10,000 in approx 1910; 15,000 in approx 1940; 20,000 in approx 2000. **2a)** 1878 **b)** 1858 **c)** 1987 **d)** 1969 **e)** 1887 **f)** 1860. **3)** From top to bottom: 1850; 1854; 1858; 1860; 1878; 1885; 1887; 1902; 1910; 1940; 1969; 1987; 2000. **p20 1)** 3 roundabouts **2)** Church with spire **3)** It follows the curve of the coast/shore/beach/bay **4)** south-west **5)** 7882 **6)** 207 m **7)** Visitor Centre **8)** approx 778 827 **9)** It would take about 15 minutes **10)** 7781 is a housing area whilst 7882 is mainly shops/hotels and public buildings. **p23 1)** 'Central' because it's in the middle of town; 'Business' because this is the main land use found there; 'District' is a word which describes a district or area of a town. **3)** The main land use of the area is for shopping but offices, houses and catering are also important. **p27 2)** Example answers – Overnight stays: Only 12% of all visitors stayed overnight; this means that only about 1/8 (or 1 in 8) of all visitors stayed more than one day; Travel to Llandudno: Most visitors (75%) travelled by car; fewest people (6%) arrived by train; About 1 in 5 people travelled by bus or coach; Where visitors lived: The single biggest group came from NW England – which is the nearest region in England to Llandudno; More people came from NW England than came from Wales; which came second; However the third largest group came from one of the furthest regions – the SE of England. **p28 ACROSS** 2 Chester 6 Economic Activity 7 Traffic 8 Survey 10 Isobar 12 Tombolo 13 Trail 14 Chart 16 Limestone 17 O.S. 19 Landscape 21 Tram 22 Pier 25 Orme 26 Sea 28 Snowdonia 31 Shop 32 Beaches 33 Access. **DOWN** 1 Great 2 Cliffs 3 Route 4 Location 5 Street plan 8 Sub 9 Forecast 11 Services 15 Railway 18 National 20 Atlas 23 Romans 24 New 26 Scale 27 Copper 29 Buoys 30 C.B.D.

O.S. symbols

Symbol	Meaning of symbol	Symbol	Meaning of symbol
M1	Motorway	🏛	Museum
A30	Main road	🏰	English Heritage castle
B3074	Secondary road		National Trust property
	Minor road	Ⓚ	Recreation/leisure/sports centre
– – –	Bridleway		Caravan site
· · · ·	Footpath	Λ	Camping site
◆ ◆ ◆	National trail or long distance footpath	✕	Picnic site
· · ·	Other routes with public access	✆	Telephone box
❗	Walks/trails	⌐	Golf course
🚲	Cycle trail	CH	Club house
━●━	Railway track and station	U	Horse riding
🚂	Preserved railway		Nature reserve
FB	Footbridge	☀	Viewpoint
P	Parking	Ⓨ	Country park
P&R	Park and ride parking	☆	Other tourist attraction
	Building	Hut Circle	Pre-Roman antiquity
PO	Post office		River
	Public house		Stream
▲	Youth hostel		Lake
V	Visitor centre	◦W	Well
𝑖	Information centre	Spr	Spring
♁	Place of worship with a tower		Marsh
♂	Place of worship with a spire, minaret or dome	50	Contour (at 50 m intervals)
†	Other place of worship	• 201	Spot height (at 201 m)
	Bus and coach station		Woodland
𝚇	Mast	⌒⌒⌒	Cliff
✗	Windmill		Sandy beach
𝚇	Wind pump or generator		Bracken, heath or rough grassland
⊸⊸⊸	Electricity transmission line with pylons	♨	Lighthouse
TH	Town hall	⚔ 1066	Site of a battle